IMAGES
of America

Forestry Sciences Lab in Mercer County

In 1961, the US Forest Service worked with Pres. John F. Kennedy to develop a center for the scientific study of marketing and enhancing the hardwood forests of the Appalachian Mountain region. The architectural firm of Zando, Martin & Milstead prepared this drawing of the proposed center on May 4, 1962. (Courtesy of the US Forest Service.)

On the Cover: A 19th-century logging crew works near Mill Creek in Coopers, West Virginia. (Courtesy of Grubb Photo Service.)

IMAGES
of America

FORESTRY SCIENCES LAB IN MERCER COUNTY

William R. "Bill" Archer

ARCADIA PUBLISHING

ISBN 978-1-4671-0608-5

Published by Arcadia Publishing
Charleston, South Carolina

Printed in the United States of America

Library of Congress Control Number: 2020944087

For all general information, please contact Arcadia Publishing:
Telephone 843-853-2070
Fax 843-853-0044
E-mail sales@arcadiapublishing.com
For customer service and orders:
Toll-Free 1-888-313-2665

Visit us on the Internet at www.arcadiapublishing.com

I dedicate this book to the memory of my late wife,
Evonda Louise Archer (December 30, 1951–October 3, 2019),
my inspiration, soulmate, and the love of my life.

Contents

Acknowledgments

On January 2, 2017, the first official day of my term as a Mercer County commissioner, I set out to see what could be done to restore the Mercer County Poor Farm Cemetery. From 1918 until 1951, the county provided the basic essentials of life to untold hundreds of poor souls—White and Black, male and female, young and old. The ones who died at the poor farm were buried in mostly unmarked graves in a hilltop cemetery near the farm. When I arrived that day, I learned that the facility had closed.

When I returned to the commission office, I started the process of getting access to the cemetery. Mercer County administrator Vicky Reed put me in contact with Betsy Porterfield, who had worked at the US Department of Agriculture (USDA) Forestry Sciences Laboratory but was then assigned to a nearby US Forest Service facility. Reed has assisted with this effort every step of the way. Betsy Porterfield also assisted and put me in contact with Dr. Sokjae Cho, director of the US Forest Service Northern Research Station, who told me that the General Services Administration (GSA) had possession of the property. GSA staff, including Kristine Carson, Perry Gibbs, and Warren Frazier, along with Sarah Killinger and John Barrett of the National Park Service and Neal Bennett of the US Forest Service, who took over after Porterfield retired, all helped.

I would also like to thank Charles "Tom" Cover, director of the West Virginia Division of Forestry; Chris White of the southern West Virginia office of the Division of Forestry; Bert Ulrich of the NASA Office of Communications; John Larson of the Polson Museum in Hoqulam, Washington; and Samuel H. Gardner, Grant Bennett, and Dominic Cumberland of the US Forest Service.

I would also like to thank Mercer County Commission president Gene Buckner and my fellow commissioner Greg Puckett, as well as Mercer County clerk Verlin Moye and staff members Debbie Brewster and Tammy Zigler. Thanks also to Jason Roberts and Jeff Johnson of Region One, Appalachian Region Commission, along with Todd Gray and Todd Kendall, both of the Mercer County Assessor's Office. Thanks to Amy Lester of the Mercer County Fire Board; David Longwood, Donald G. Cuppett Jr., and all the former employees of the USDA Forestry Sciences Laboratory; and the people of Mercer County.

Introduction

The true excitement of history often emerges quietly when the trails of discovery merge and the complex matrix of seemingly unconnected dots align to form a perfect circle. In the spring of 1960, during a hard-fought presidential primary campaign, Sen. John F. Kennedy was able to mentally unravel the complex social history of the Appalachian region and see a way for it to set sail on a new course. While many previous leaders and entrepreneurs couldn't see the forest for the trees, Kennedy saw the future in the woods of Appalachia and set a postelection course that would fulfill that vision.

During Kennedy's campaign for the Democratic Party's presidential nomination, a trio of old-school southern West Virginia politicians—Broughton Johnston, Laurence Tierney, and Sydney Christy—formed the nucleus of Kennedy's coalfield campaign. Johnston brought in a young lawyer, Robert E. Holroyd, to show Kennedy around Mercer County. One of their stops was the abandoned poor farm. Holroyd enjoyed visiting the Mercer County Poor Farm in his youth, when his father, Dr. Frank Holroyd, contracted with the Mercer County Commission to care for the poor farm's sick and injured. On that tour, Kennedy saw the cleared 200-acre poor farm site, which bordered on the new West Virginia Turnpike in the very heart of Appalachia.

Kennedy was not the first future US president to visit the site. During the Civil War, Lt. Col. Rutherford B. Hayes of the 64th Ohio Volunteer Infantry Regiment and Pvt. William McKinley pushed through that same ground on their way to meeting Confederate forces in the May 1862 Battle of Pigeon's Roost in Princeton, West Virginia. After his election, Kennedy assembled the governors of eight Appalachian states in the White House in May 1961 to develop a strategy to address the problem of generational poverty in the region. By that September, Kennedy had persuaded North American Aviation to invest nearly $1 million to build a component production facility in Princeton. On October 12, 1961, the Mercer County Commission transferred the title of the former poor farm to the US Forest Service to erect an experimental forest products lab.

Kennedy selected a budding forestry scientist, Franklin R. "Frank" Longwood, to head up the project, and Longwood selected a battle-tested teenaged combat pilot turned forester, Donald G. Cuppett Sr., to be his second in command. Longwood and Cuppett were both onboard before the county commission transferred the deed to the federal government. The two worked tirelessly to create a laboratory that would open new markets for timber and enhance safety for loggers, truckers, and sawyers.

Construction of the facility got underway in 1962, and the Forestry Sciences Laboratory was dedicated on November 12, 1963. Both of West Virginia's US senators, Jennings Randolph and Robert C. Byrd, participated in the dedication. Hamilton K. Pyles, deputy chief of the US Forest Service, stated that the problems and challenges of the forest had been known for many years but noted that the solutions to those problems had been addressed by "educated and uneducated guesses." He said the creation of the new laboratory should result in finding solutions to the problems. "The Princeton Laboratory should be the vanguard of this movement," Pyles said.

"While we attend this ceremony, the president's Appalachian Regional Commission, headed by Franklin D. Roosevelt Jr., is meeting with Governor [Bert T.] Combs and key people from the state of Kentucky to discuss proposals for improving the economic situation of Appalachia," Pyles stated. "One of the major items of the commission will be discussing during the next two weeks, not only in Kentucky but in all Appalachian states, is a solution to problems involved in the utilization and marketing of the region's timber." Pyles concluded his remarks with this comment: "This facility can play a significant role in the massive thrust that is needed to improve the overall economy of this mountainous and forested region of Appalachia."

Just 10 days after Pyles delivered these remarks, the nation was mourning the November 22, 1963, assassination of President Kennedy. Still, Kennedy had planted the seeds, and Longwood and Cuppett labored tirelessly to fulfill the promise of Kennedy's hope for the Appalachian region. The team worked with a growing legion of forestry scientists that eventually numbered about 60. The forestry experts needed a support staff of nearly 100 to generate the data and develop innovative systems. Sadly, Frank Longwood died on September 28, 1966, but he had already set the wheels in motion. The US Forest Service selected Cuppett to serve as director of the facility, and by the mid-1970s, the programs had grown to such an extent that the laboratory facility had to be expanded.

In the fall of 1975, active research programs at the lab included a practical system for weighing truckloads of saw-logs; a computerized system of determining log values to help lumber producers and evaluate sawmill productivity; developing new designs for logging trucks to more adequately distribute load weights; a forced-air circulation method to pre-dry hardwoods that cut drying times by two thirds with less drying degrade; new uses for bark residues, including mulch for erosion control and vegetative cover at highway construction sites, surface mine reclamation, and in greenhouses; applications for hardwood use in plywood manufacturing; a pallet exchange system from low-grade hardwood logs to handle bulk mail for the US Postal Service and Sears, Roebuck & Co.; a pallet repair program; a comprehensive, cost-effective safety program to reduce injury and accident incidents at sawmill and logging operations; recommendations to stabilize sawmill and logging workforces by encouraging paid holiday and other financial incentives; providing statistical data to assist Christmas tree growers and marketers; developing standards for using hardwoods for highway guardrail posts; and developing a rough mill design for efficient processing of low-grade yellow poplar lumber for interior furniture parts.

The dedication of the new wing of the facility on October 18, 1975, brought two of President Kennedy's dreams together: helping people of the Appalachian region and sending a man to the moon. On May 25, 1961, Kennedy had announced his plan to send a man to the moon and return him to earth safely. While he did not live to see that dream fulfilled, the dreams merged in 1971, when astronaut Stuart Rosa, a former US Forest Service smoke jumper, carried tree seeds to the moon on Apollo 14 as part of a joint NASA/US Forest Service adventure. Once germinated, the Forest Service distributed "Moon Tree" saplings nationwide as part of the 1976 US bicentennial celebration.

Donald G. Cuppett had been the driving force behind the lab's work following Longwood's death, but on January 10, 1983, he was killed in a two-vehicle accident. Other forestry scientists followed, but with increasing global competition in forestry, the United States' approach to scientific forestry changed. Staffing levels declined, and in September 2016, the lab was shuttered. The Mercer County Commission received the property from the General Services Administration through the National Park Service's Historic Surplus Properties Program on February 12, 2020. A new chapter now begins.

One

From Lumber Harvest to Hope

The sycamore tree in this 20th-century photograph was thought to be one of the last examples of the virgin timber forest that early settlers saw upon arrival. The tree, shown here surrounded by a fence, was located near Elk Lick in Webster County. (Courtesy of the US Forest Service.)

In 1906–1907, E.L. Gardner, president of Bluestone Lumber Company, located a band saw lumbermill on the banks of Brush Creek in Mercer County. Gardner acquired approximately 170 acres for the operation, which he called Sharp's Camp. He also acquired easement rights-of-way for a narrow-gauge logging railroad. Gardner gave the property to Bluestone Lumber Company executives, who later sold the rights to the Mercer County Commission. (Courtesy of Samuel H. Gardner.)

E.L. Gardner sold Bluestone's band saw to an unknown Pacific Northwest lumbermill in 1917. This photograph shows a band saw crew working at a mill in that region. John Larson, director of a logging museum in Hoqulam, Washington, shared this photograph with the Mercer County Commission. (Courtesy of the Polson Museum.)

Loggers harvested timber from Flat Top Mountain along with other properties in Mercer County. Most of the lumber processed at Sharp's Camp went to the construction of the Virginian Railway and the structures associated with that massive infrastructure project. Henry Huttleston Rogers launched his railroad in 1902 and completed the line from Norfolk, Virginia, to Deepwater, West Virginia, in 1909. The mill produced lumber for the company towns that emerged near coalmine operations along the route. (Courtesy of Samuel H. Gardner.)

Lumbermills like this operation in the Pacific Northwest processed timber in various sizes to meet the needs of customers. Mine operators who bought lumber from Bluestone Lumber Company needed hardwoods for use as mine cribbing to support the tops and ribs of mines as well as boards for housing and company offices. The Virginian Railway followed its neighbor, the Norfolk & Western Railway, in about 20 years, at a time when industrial technology was advancing rapidly. (Courtesy of the Polson Museum.)

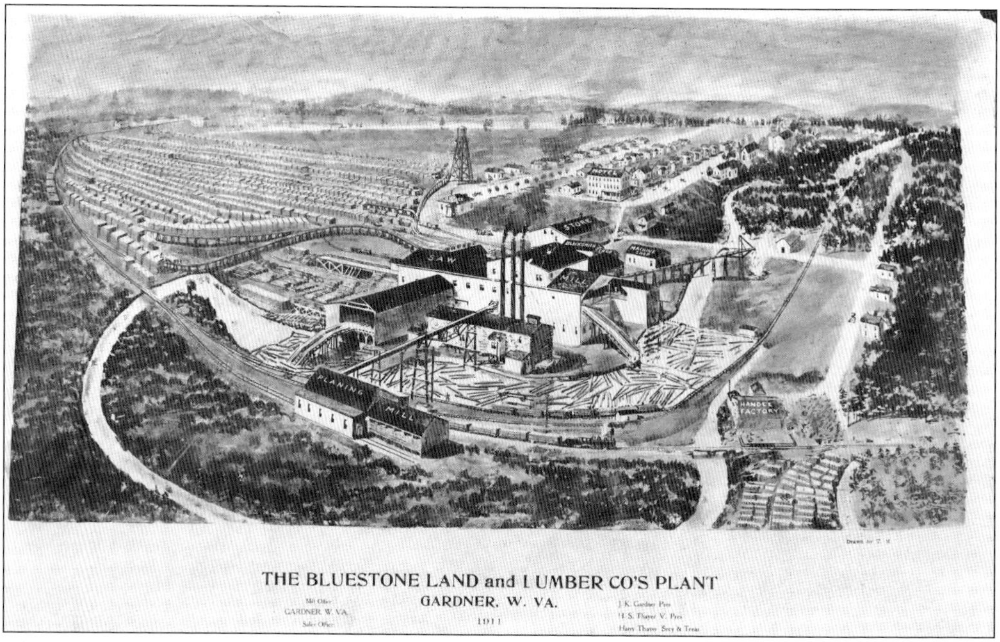

The Bluestone Lumber Company grew quickly, and the band saw processed acres of lumber for the Virginian Railway and mining operations in Mercer and Wyoming Counties in West Virginia. Mining towns like Matoaka in Mercer County, Mullens in Wyoming County, and Slab Fork in Raleigh County grew quickly. While coal was the primary export, people with roots in the coalfields also made themselves known. Singer-songwriter Bill Withers was born in Slab Fork. (Reproduction by Grant Bennett.)

It took manpower to operate Bluestone Lumber's huge band saw operation, and since the mill was in Mercer County farmlands, Bluestone provided housing for its employees. The boardinghouse housed unmarried laborers, while workers with families lived in the duplex houses of Sharp's Camp. The buildings were hastily assembled and, according to families that grew up in the duplex homes, were poorly insulated. (Courtesy of Samuel H. Gardner.)

Bluestone managers and supervisors enjoyed slightly better housing, like the single-family home shown here. After E.L. Gardner sold the band saw to a buyer in the Pacific Northwest and the land to the Mercer County Commission, he gave the logging railway right-of-way to the company's top executives. A few years later, they sold the right-of-way to the county commission as well. (Courtesy of the Mercer County Commission Archives.)

E.L. Gardner sold the property as well as the existing houses to the Mercer County Commission in 1917. In the following few months, the commission rehabilitated some of the houses as well as the boardinghouse to provide shelter to homeless individuals and families. The commission opened the Mercer County Poor Farm in 1918, and while records are few, some residents familiar with the poor farm estimated its population to be between 300 and 375 people during the Great Depression. (Courtesy of the Mercer County Commission Archives.)

Much of the timber produced at the Bluestone Lumber band saw operation went to support coalmine operations like the Crane Creek Mine, shown here. Crane Creek began producing coal with miners like these in 1902, but in a few years, American Coal Company acquired Crane Creek and other nearby mines. The work was dangerous, but the mostly metallurgical coal produced there helped build the United States into an industrial superpower. (Courtesy of Grubb Photo Service.)

While coal miners earned a living, sometimes their families suffered loss when accidents due to engineering mistakes led to fatalities. On June 9, 1924, a massive gob pile at the Crane Creek Mine gave way following several days of heavy rain, killing seven residents and one rescuer. When coal-mining families suffered the loss of family members or housing, they often had nowhere else to turn except the county poor farm. (Courtesy of Grubb Photo Service.)

Two sawyers with a Civilian Conservation Corps (CCC) camp in 1935 are whipsawing cedar boards to be used at a CCC camp in Lewis County, Washington, at Gifford Pinchot National Forest. Gifford Pinchot was among the nation's leading foresters. In 1898, Pres. William McKinley appointed Pinchot to serve as the first director of the US Forest Service. In one of those odd quirks of fate, President McKinley had served in the 64th Ohio Volunteer Infantry Regiment, which was stationed at Camp Jones on Flat Top Mountain in Mercer County, then part of Virginia, in April 1862. McKinley rose to the rank of sergeant at Camp Jones, where he served under Lt. Col. Rutherford B. Hayes. In May 1862, the 64th Ohio Infantry marched through what would become the Mercer County Poor Farm on its way to the Battle of Pigeon Roost in Princeton. (Courtesy of the US Forest Service.)

Using the labor of poor farm residents, Superintendent Thomas Clayton Hedrick successfully upgraded the boardinghouse. Along with making much-needed improvements to their quarters, poor farm residents—male and female of all races, creeds, and nations of origin—grew their own crops and raised their own cattle and pigs. During construction of the 1930 Mercer County Courthouse, the county commission salvaged the old courthouse bell and took it to the poor farm to call workers from the fields. (Courtesy of the Mercer County Commission Archives.)

The Great Depression caused many hardships for families throughout the United States, and the coalfields of southern West Virginia witnessed their share of problems. Workers from regional CCC camps came to the Mercer County Poor Farm and erected single-family cabins to help address that challenge. During that time, it was not unusual for Superintendent Hedrick to drive truckloads of poor farm men to the office of Dr. Frank J. Holroyd in Princeton to receive treatment for venereal disease. (Courtesy of the Mercer County Commission Archives.)

During the post–World War II era, foresters looked to the nation's woodlands to transform a wartime economy back into peacetime productivity. Frank Longwood, a farm forester who would later be a research forester at the Central States Forest Experiment Station in Ames, Iowa, is shown there around 1945 tallying a plot of bottomland forest. Longwood earned his bachelor's degree in forestry from Michigan State University in 1938 and his master's degree in forestry from Oregon State University in 1940. During the war, he served as a fire dispatcher at the Manistee National Forest in Michigan, and after the war, he rose through the forestry ranks and authored two books regarded as classics in the forestry field. (Courtesy of David Longwood.)

With a growing reliance on trucks to harvest timber in West Virginia, the job of mountain loggers became increasingly challenging. This view of a precarious Logan County logging road about 20 miles from Man, West Virginia, shows one of the many difficulties lumber workers faced getting their timber to the sawmill. (Courtesy of the US Forest Service.)

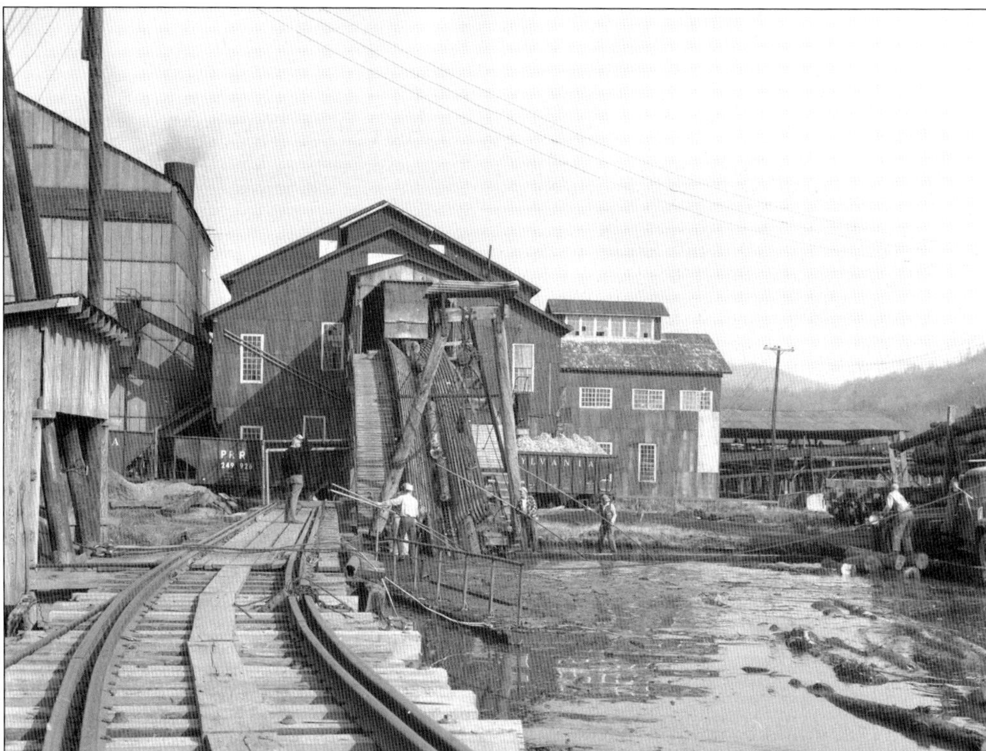

As timber processing technology advanced, the challenges faced by workers remained constant. Sawmill workers at the Meadow River Lumber Company mill in Rainelle, Greenbrier County, West Virginia, are shown as they move logs into the mill. (Courtesy of the US Forest Service.)

A worker is observing the cut of a spruce log on the head saw at the Columbia Lumber Company mill at Sitka, Baranof Island, Alaska. Leland J. Prater took this photograph in 1958. The log was harvested from the northern Tongess National Forest in Alaska. (Courtesy of the US Forest Service.)

Smaller logs at the Meadow River Lumber Company sawmill were processed in the same way the larger logs are processed on a big band saw. The workers shown here had an awesome responsibility to prepare the logs for market. (Courtesy of the US Forest Service.)

A sawyer prepares to guide a log through the head saw at the Curtis Lumber Mill on State Route 10 in Springfield, Virginia. Bluford W. Muir took this photograph at the mill in 1946. (Courtesy of the US Forest Service.)

A worker saws an oak log taken from the Jefferson National Forest timber sale in 1955 at the J.B. Belcher & Son Mill at Natural Bridge, Virginia. Leland J. Prater was the photographer. (Courtesy of the US Forest Service.)

This huge "cookie" saw cut has been on display for many years in the lobby of the USDA Forestry Sciences Laboratory in Gardner. The log was harvested from the Neely Farm in Mercer County in the fall of 1972 during construction of Interstate 77 and US Route 460. The Appalachian white oak tree was about 23 years old at the start of the French and Indian War in 1754. The cookie was moved to the Robert C. Byrd Hardwood Center when the forestry lab closed in 2016. (Photograph by Grant Bennett.)

US senator John F. Kennedy greets a Mercer County resident during the county Democratic Party Bean Dinner on April 26, 1960. Senator Kennedy was stumping for votes in the West Virginia primary election in May. He was in a hotly contested race with US senator Hubert H. Humphrey of Minnesota. The party leaders connected with the youthful New Englander and championed his campaign. After he won the primary, Kennedy selected Robert E. "Bob" Holroyd, a young Mercer County attorney, to serve as his southern West Virginia campaign chair. Holroyd and his twin brother, Fred, enjoyed many visits to the Mercer County Poor Farm with their father, Dr. Frank J. Holroyd. The well-known Princeton doctor enjoyed visiting the poor farm at mealtime because of the excellent cooks who lived at the farm, according to Bob Holroyd. (Photograph by Melvin Grubb, courtesy of Grubb Photo Service.)

Two

Kennedy's West Virginia Primary Pledge

The Mercer County Commission closed the poor farm in 1951 and started working with a goal of selling the property and bringing it back into the tax rolls. In the late 1950s, the commission went as far as attempting to sell the property at auction but considered the lone $16,000 bid unacceptable. Even with the opening of the West Virginia Turnpike in 1955, no serious investors took interest. (Courtesy of the Mercer County Commission Archives.)

Photographer Vernon Fields seems to have been more interesting to his wife, Helen, than who she was shaking hands with when Senator Kennedy was campaigning in April 1960. Fields had been seriously wounded in the Korean War and was working part-time for Grubb Photo Service. Grubb processed film and provided news photographs to the *Bluefield Daily Telegraph*. The newspaper kept the photograph on file but did not use it because Helen was looking at the photographer. The image is significant because Kennedy is standing beside his friend and ally Franklin Delano Roosevelt Jr. Both men were US Navy officers during World War II. FDR Jr. campaigned tirelessly for Kennedy, and when the president decided to use his position to address the problem of generational poverty in the Appalachian region, he selected Roosevelt to chair the commission. (Courtesy of the *Bluefield Daily Telegraph*.)

Senator Kennedy and his wife, Jacqueline Bouvier Kennedy, are shown at the April 26, 1960, Mercer County Democratic Party Bean Dinner at the county 4-H camp in Glenwood Park. Jacqueline Kennedy's family had historic ties to both forestry and southern West Virginia. Her great-grandfather Michael Bouvier was a cabinetmaker in Philadelphia who in 1834 headed up an investment company that acquired a large tract of land in Mercer and McDowell Counties. (Courtesy of the *Bluefield Daily Telegraph*.)

Senator Kennedy made several trips to southern West Virginia during his 1960 presidential campaign. Melvin Grubb took this photograph of Kennedy meeting with students of Bluefield State College, one of two historically Black colleges in West Virginia. The meeting took place in the auditorium in Gilbert Hall. (Courtesy of Grubb Photo Service.)

Less than four months after his inauguration, President Kennedy invited the governors of eight Appalachian states to a luncheon meeting at the White House. From left to right are North Carolina governor Terry Sanford, Virginia governor J. Lindsay Almond Jr., Tennessee governor Buford Ellington, Kentucky governor Bert T. Combs, Kennedy, Pennsylvania governor David L. Lawrence, Maryland governor J. Millard Tawes, Alabama governor John Patterson, and West Virginia governor William W. Barron. According to a press release from the White House, President Kennedy directed the Area Redevelopment Administration to focus attention on the region with respect to worker retraining, Defense Department contracts, and other areas. "It is the first time an entire section of a nation has been organized to develop an important regional program of this magnitude," Kennedy stated. (Courtesy of Abbie Rowe, White House Photographs, John F. Kennedy Presidential Library and Museum.)

The southern Appalachian Mountains touch 13 states: New York, Pennsylvania, Ohio, West Virginia, Maryland, Virginia, Kentucky, Tennessee, North Carolina, South Carolina, Georgia, Alabama, and Mississippi. West Virginia is the only state that is entirely within the mountain range. The challenge of generational poverty that President Kennedy recognized during his campaign in 1960 still exists in many states in the region 60 years later, but the seeds of change that Kennedy planted in the spring of 1961 continue to bear fruit through modern infrastructure projects, educational and healthcare facilities, and even the NASA space program, part of which took root in Huntsville, Alabama. From its humble origins, the Appalachian Region Commission continues to bring positive change to this economically challenged area. The Forestry Sciences Lab is indicated by the star. (Courtesy of the Appalachian Region Commission.)

The opening of the Memorial Tunnel on the West Virginia Turnpike in the early 1950s signaled the start of increased access to southern West Virginia. When it was built, the tunnel featured television cameras that monitored traffic flow, ventilation exhaust fans, and water hydrants for fire protection. President Kennedy would have traveled through this tunnel during his 1960 campaign. (Courtesy of the West Virginia Parkways Authority.)

The two-lane Memorial Tunnel was built for $5 million and "dedicated to all West Virginians who have served or are now serving in the Armed Forces of the United States." While the tunnel was closed in the 1980s, it has been used for both civilian and military training exercises in recent years. (Courtesy of the West Virginia Parkways Authority.)

The Glass House snack bar was a welcome rest stop for motorists traveling the West Virginia Turnpike. The rest area is still located on the southeast side of the Bluestone Gorge about two miles from the site where President Kennedy envisioned construction of the Forestry Sciences Laboratory. (Courtesy of the West Virginia Parkways Authority.)

The Charlton Memorial Bridge over the Bluestone Gorge towers 246 feet above the Bluestone River. When the turnpike opened in 1955, the bridge was dedicated to West Virginian Sgt. Cornelius Charlton, one of only two African Americans to receive the Medal of Honor during the Korean War. Charlton was killed in action in 1951. (Courtesy of the West Virginia Parkways Authority.)

Donald G. Cuppett Sr. employed a hands-on approach to forestry work. A Preston County, West Virginia, native, Cuppett graduated from Terra Alta High School in 1943 and entered the military during World War II, when he piloted B-25 Mitchell, A-26, and C-46 aircraft in the US Army Air Corps. After his discharge from active duty, Cuppett remained with the West Virginia Air National Guard until he retired. He earned a degree from the West Virginia University School of Forestry in 1946 and served as an assistant state forester until he took a job as manager of a sawmill in Spencer, West Virginia, owned by Union Carbide Corporation. After relocating to Mercer County in 1962 to work at the Forestry Sciences Lab, Cuppett earned a reputation as one of the nation's top forestry scientists. (Courtesy of the US Forest Service.)

Preparing sawn lumber for sale is both an art and a science. Frank Longwood is shown here examining a cottonwood lumber stack at the Bergen Brothers sawmill in Ames, Iowa. Longwood went to Ames as a farm forester, but he was soon promoted to research forester with the Central States Forest Experiment Station there. (Courtesy of David Longwood.)

By the mid-1950s, Frank Longwood had also earned a reputation as one of the top forestry scientists in the United States. In 1954, he was appointed to serve as project leader at the Tropical Forest Experiment Station at Rio Piedras, Puerto Rico. Here he examines tropical wood drying at the experiment station. (Courtesy of David Longwood.)

Frank Longwood (far left) and two unidentified men are examining the start of construction at the Forestry Sciences Laboratory in 1962. President Kennedy selected Longwood to serve as the director of the facility in September 1961. At the time, Longwood was serving as research leader at the Northeastern Forest Experiment Station in Brewer, Maine. Longwood selected West Virginian Donald G. Cuppett Sr. to be his second in command, and the two men began designing a facility that would support a scientific approach to opening new markets for forest products. The work of creating the facility started prior to October 12, 1961, before the Mercer County Commission transferred the property to the federal government. (Courtesy of the US Forest Service.)

Three

The Scientific Approach to Forestry

Once the nine-acre site had been cleared, work on the Forestry Sciences Laboratory got underway. The Charleston, West Virginia–based architectural firm of Zando, Martin & Milstead Inc. completed the blueprints on May 4, 1962, and work got underway. The original structure was all on one level and included 13,000 square feet of space. (Courtesy of the US Forest Service.)

Although there is an entrance to the lobby of the Forestry Sciences Lab on the northwest side of the building, the primary lobby entrance is on the southeast side of the building, shown here. The cornerstone to the right dedicated the structure to President Kennedy in 1962. (Courtesy of the US Forest Service.)

The parking lot is located in the rear of the lab facility. As a result, even when the entire complement of scientists and staff are present, the view of the front of the building is unobstructed by the sight of vehicles. The initial parking lot was expanded during the lab expansion project in 1975. (Courtesy of the US Forest Service.)

Zando, Martin & Milstead selected a young architect, Edward Theodore "Ted" Boggess, to serve as contract administrator on the Forestry Sciences Lab project. Boggess was from Charleston, served in the US Navy during the Korean War, and earned his architectural degree from the Ohio State University. He settled in Mercer County, established a highly successful architectural firm, and was a dedicated community servant until his passing in 2019. (Courtesy of E.T. Boggess Architect Inc.)

One of the "cool" features of the Forestry Sciences Lab building is the feature shown here near the main entrance on the east side of the structure. During the summer months, the feature deflects the sun's rays, making the entrance cooler, while in the winter months, it directs the sunlight toward the building for solar warming. (Courtesy of the US Forest Service.)

The garage structure was initially designed as a six-bay facility, but prior to completion, a seventh double bay was added on the north end of the building to provide lumber storage. The double bay on the south end was used as a woodworking shop where skilled craftsmen fashioned some of the furnishings. (Courtesy of the US Forest Service.)

While the north-end double bay was used primarily for lumber storage, after acquiring the facility in the winter of 2020, the Mercer County Commission is in the process of cleaning it out and using it to store personal protective equipment for regional emergency service providers. Mercer County serves as an emergency PPE distribution site for three southern West Virginia counties. (Photograph by the author.)

Two workers are erecting a storage building associated with the Forest Service's methods testing facility on Cornbread Ridge. The main methods testing facility was not finished when the Forestry Sciences Lab was dedicated on November 12, 1963. (Courtesy of the US Forest Service.)

The methods testing plant served as a facility where scientists at the Forestry Sciences Lab could test their innovations in a real-life setting. The plant was erected on the site where the Bluestone Lumber band saw operated. Forest Service staff stated that the builders had to dig through 10 to 12 feet of sawdust before reaching solid ground. (Courtesy of the US Forest Service.)

The large feature at right is the 150-seat auditorium where scientists explained the concepts of the projects they were working on to their colleagues; it also hosted public gatherings. Skilled contractors built the structure to the unique requirements of Frank Longwood and Donald G. Cuppett Sr. (Courtesy of the US Forest Service.)

The auditorium was designed to celebrate Appalachian hardwoods with numerous displays highlighting the many uses for hardwoods harvested in the forests. The auditorium features oak parquet flooring and cherry hardwood paneling. Both woods are indigenous to the Appalachian region. (Courtesy of the US Forest Service.)

The Forestry Sciences Lab featured a kitchenette next to the auditorium to provide meals to guests attending functions at the lab. One unique feature of the kitchen is a built-in combination sink, stovetop, and refrigerator. (Photograph by the author.)

Visitors to the lobby of the Forestry Sciences Lab got the opportunity to test their ability to identify the leaves of trees native to the Appalachian region and the grain of the trees' wood. Skilled woodworkers crafted the device, which remains fully operational. (Photograph by the author.)

Each of the offices in the original building prior to the 1975 addition features hardwood paneling made from a variety of tree species harvested from the Appalachian region. Office 133, shown here, features mahogany paneling. (Photograph by the author.)

The solar-inspired architectural feature shown here shielded employees who worked in the secretarial pool from the heat of summer sun but drew the warming powers of the sun during the winter. A dozen or more secretaries provided clerical support to the approximately 60 scientists working at the lab. (Photograph by the author.)

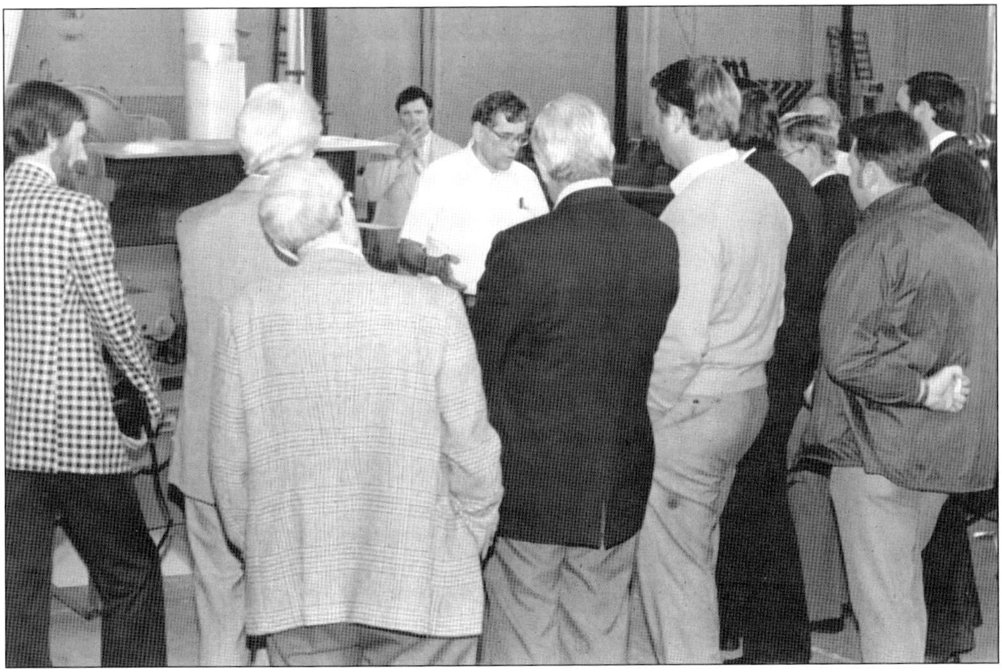

Hugh Reynolds of the Forestry Sciences Lab explains a process to visitors in the methods testing plant. When scientists came up with innovative uses for hardwoods or new safety practices, they tested their theories in the plant before sharing their ideas with the forestry community. (Courtesy of the US Forest Service.)

Edward L. Adams, forest products technologist (left), and Neal D. Bennett, physical science technologist, are conducting a test on a CNC (computer numerical control) router in the methods testing plant. (Courtesy of the US Forest Service.)

The methods testing plant is shown here soon after its construction. Employees at the plant continue to conduct testing on hardwood application projects. (Courtesy of the US Forest Service.)

The fencing around the air seasoning stock was erected to reduce the effects of rain and direct sunlight. This was just one of the many ongoing projects conducted by the staff of the methods testing plant. (Courtesy of the US Forest Service.)

Tragedy struck the Forestry Sciences Lab on September 28, 1966, when Frank Longwood died suddenly while visiting an office in Princeton. Longwood's death prompted US senator Robert C. Byrd to place a tribute in the Congressional Record on October 12, 1966. Byrd stated that the Forestry Sciences Laboratory had been in the vanguard of research to uncover new uses for domestic timbers thanks to Longwood. "Although he will be succeeded by another highly competent research engineer, Mr. Donald G. Cuppett, I believe the laboratory will long benefit from the administrative organization which Mr. Longwood created at Princeton." With President Kennedy's assassination on November 22, 1963—just days after the lab was dedicated—and Longwood's death less than three years later, the Forestry Sciences Laboratory experienced great loss during its formative years. (Courtesy of the US Forest Service.)

After contractors released the facility to the Forest Service, the parking lot began to fill up with scientists and support staff. As the success of the project grew, the managers needed to review the possibility of expanding the facility. (Courtesy of the US Forest Service.)

The first phase of the garage project was completed prior to the November 12, 1963, dedication of the complex. Like the lab itself, the garage was declared a historic building by the General Services Administration, the National Park Service, and the West Virginia State Historic Preservation Office. (Courtesy of the US Forest Service.)

The scientists of the Forestry Sciences Laboratory were likely attracted to the field of research because of their love of trees. The foresters developed a rock-lined trail system through the approximately 23 acres of woodlands on the property that the Mercer County Commission gave the Forest Service in 1961. (Courtesy of the US Forest Service.)

The woodland trails extend more than three miles through the forest. The main trail leads to the Poor Farm Cemetery, which includes about 250 mostly unmarked graves. Other trails lead past rock outcroppings and other fascinating features. (Courtesy of the US Forest Service.)

Loggers used horsepower and mule power to get logs to lumber mills in the mid-20th century, and the scientists of the Forestry Sciences Laboratory were dedicated to opening up new markets for those products as well as developing safer ways to harvest the hardwoods. (Courtesy of the US Forest Service.)

West Virginia, and indeed the entire Appalachian region, was poised to become one of the most successful hardwood-producing areas in the world. With the opening of new markets and improvements to safety and equipment, the industry was about to emerge. (Courtesy of the US Forest Service.)

Four

EXPANDING FOREST PRODUCTS MARKETS

It's beginning to look a lot like Christmas trees in this field at an unknown location. The scientists of the Forestry Sciences Lab at Gardner tackled a myriad of approaches to opening markets for forest products, including assisting farmers to sell Christmas trees. The US Forest Service continues to play a role in that industry. (Courtesy of the US Forest Service.)

During the 1960s, the Forest Service took a leadership role in securing and transporting the national Christmas tree that is displayed annually on the Ellipse in Washington, DC. Forest Service workers are shown securing a tree prior to felling. Although the location of the tree in this photograph is unknown, the national Christmas tree in 1963 came from West Virginia. The official tree-lighting ceremony had been delayed until December 22, 1963, the day that the national period of mourning following the assassination of President Kennedy concluded. The ground in Washington was snow-covered during the ceremony, just as it was when the tree was felled. (Courtesy of the US Forest Service.)

After securing the 71-foot Norway (red) spruce tree, foresters started the challenging task of felling the tree so the base would be stable after it was transported to Washington, DC. The derrick operator (far right) took pressure off the cut as the sawyers completed their work. (Courtesy of the US Forest Service.)

Specialized freight carrier Hemingway Transport Inc., based in New Bedford, Massachusetts, with offices in Philadelphia, Washington, DC, and elsewhere, transported the 71-foot tree to its final destination. (Courtesy of the US Forest Service.)

The Norwegian spruce from West Virginia was decorated with 8,000 lights courtesy of a decades-long tradition from General Electric Company. Pres. Lyndon B. Johnson lit the tree at 6:30 p.m. on December 22, 1963, bringing an end to the month-long national period of mourning in honor of President Kennedy. While in the prior two years, pageant decorators used green dye to make the Ellipse look fresh, the blanket of snow in 1963 negated that necessity. The US Postal Service issued a stamp in 2010 recognizing 40 years of the national Christmas tree. In 1970, the Capitol architect asked the US Forest Service to assist with securing the national Christmas tree. The trees come from Forest Service–managed lands, and the Capitol architect—now Brett Blanton—personally selects the tree. (Courtesy of the US Forest Service.)

By the mid-1960s, the logging business was moving more and more into mechanization. Here, logging workers use a skid-mounted crane to load a tandem-axle straight truck at a logging operation near Abingdon, Virginia. (Courtesy of the US Forest Service.)

The scientists at the Forestry Sciences Lab concentrated a great deal of effort on transporting logs and finished lumber safely. The special log car shown here, made for the Norfolk & Western Railway, is loaded with poplar logs that will be used to manufacture veneer. This car was photographed in May 1966 in Clinchburg, Virginia. (Courtesy of the US Forest Service.)

While most truckers knew the importance of chaining down the logs on their trucks, as in this November 1966 photograph of a logging site in Man, scientists in Gardner conducted research to improve safety in log transportation and reduce injuries. (Courtesy of the US Forest Service.)

The scientists at the methods testing plant in Gardner operated fans located in a loft along the center of the building as part of the lab's forced-air dryer. The systems included heat traps suspended in the airstream below clear fiberglass panels in the roof. (Courtesy of the US Forest Service.)

Highway markings lacked any measure of uniformity in the first half of the 20th century, but scientists with the Forestry Sciences Lab developed a highway delineation system using four-by-four-inch wooden posts like the one shown here in Monterey, Virginia. (Courtesy of the US Forest Service.)

Another view of a highway delineator post, also near Monterey, demonstrates just how important a relatively simple design can be to improve auto and truck travel on the nation's highways. (Courtesy of the US Forest Service.)

A worker operates a truck-mounted auger to drill a hole to install a wooden guard post on US Route 220 near Franklin, Virginia. Scientists at the lab invented some technology and adapted existing equipment for use in new applications. (Courtesy of the US Forest Service.)

The Arrow post driver shown here was designed specifically to drive wooden guard posts into position at a roadside location. This photograph was taken at Cross Lanes, West Virginia. (Courtesy of the US Forest Service.)

The scientists at the Forestry Science Lab developed the wooden guard post program to improve traffic safety and to develop a new market for Appalachian hardwoods. The workers shown here are measuring to maintain uniformity in the placement of wooden guard posts near Prichard, West Virginia. (Courtesy of the US Forest Service.)

The measurements have been made and the auger starter hole finished, and a loader and Arrow post driver operator are preparing to place a wooden guard post near Prichard. (Courtesy of the US Forest Service.)

Workers needed to remove bark from logs during the process of manufacturing the wooden guard posts, but the scientists examined the process and came up with a brilliant way to utilize the bark and excess wood remaining after the posts were formed. (Courtesy of the US Forest Service.)

The scientists worked with industry to process the scrap bark, small limbs, and twigs into mulch. The mulch program was an important aspect of the Forestry Sciences Laboratory in the early 1970s and prompted the need to undertake an expansion project that would increase the size of the facility by more than 3,000 square feet. (Courtesy of the US Forest Service.)

The mulch produced at the Gardner facility was designed to address a challenge in coal country: the blight on the land that was left in the aftermath of large-scale surface mining. (Courtesy of the US Forest Service.)

After the coal is removed from a surface mine in the Appalachian mountain region, the exposed highwall limits post-mining uses of the land. While the federal government was addressing the issue in the early 1970s, the US Forest Service scientists found a large-scale use for the mulch on surface mine reclamation and post-highway construction projects. (Courtesy of the US Forest Service.)

In order to find new uses for secondary hardwoods—wood not used for high-end projects—the Forestry Science Laboratory team developed new markets for wood pallets like the ones being made by these workers. (Courtesy of the US Forest Service.)

The US Forest Service scientists secured a contract to supply pallets to the US Postal Service and also secured contracts in the private sector with companies including Sears, Roebuck & Company, which used the pallets for shipping its popular catalogues. (Courtesy of the US Forest Service.)

The 1975 addition expanded the size of the existing library, added an entirely new wing to the Forestry Sciences Lab with additional storage and office spaces, and increased the size of the parking lot. The addition brought the total size of the facility to 16,367 square feet. (Photograph by the author.)

John C. McGuire, chief of the US Forest Service, is shown in the auditorium at the official opening on October 18, 1975. He was the final speaker at the opening. His remarks followed the dedication address delivered by Senator Byrd. (Courtesy of the US Forest Service.)

Apollo 14 astronaut Stuart Roosa (seated, left), a US Forest Service smoke jumper before he joined the astronaut program, carried seeds with him to the moon as part of a joint NASA/US Forest Service project. Shown here with Roosa, the command module pilot, are lunar module pilot Edgar D. Mitchell (right) and mission commander Alan B. Shepard Jr. Apollo 14 was launched on January 31, 1971. (Courtesy of NASA.)

From left to right, US Forest Service chief John R. McGuire, West Virginia state forester Lester McClung, and Senator Byrd plant the seedling that was grown from one of the seeds Stuart Roosa carried with him on the Apollo 14 mission. Note the intersection of Cornbread Ridge Road and Gardner Road in the background. Chief McGuire mentioned that the tree was a sycamore. (Courtesy of the US Forest Service.)

A huge sycamore maple, flanked by two sugar maples, now grows at the site of the 1975 tree planting. While some local former and current US Forest Service employees state that the "Moon Tree" that had been planted in 1975 was unceremoniously destroyed by an employee mowing the lawn after the planting, foresters and tree biologists have confirmed that this sycamore maple appears to be about the appropriate age for a tree planted in 1975. Other seedlings grown from the seeds that traveled to the moon were distributed nationwide as part of the 1976 bicentennial celebration. Some of them have survived, but the present list of moon trees does not include any others in West Virginia. (Photograph by the author.)

Donald G. Cuppett Sr. essentially coordinated the 1975 lab expansion project and supervised the growth that contributed to the need for more space. He provided US Forest Service chief John R. McGuire with a thorough and comprehensive fact sheet of the myriad projects the Forestry Sciences Lab had addressed since 1962. From developing the pallet market to providing mulch for mine reclamation, as well as sawmill, transportation, and logging safety issues, Cuppett was the point man. He died as a result of injuries he received on Brickyard Road as he was driving to the lab early Sunday morning, January 9, 1983. According to an article in the February 1983 issue of *Nor'easter*, a publication of the US Forest Service Northeastern Station, Cuppett was "regarded as the leading specialist in the design and operation of sawing and processing facilities." He originated a method of low-temperature drying for Appalachian hardwoods, authored articles on kiln drying and sawmill operations, was a member of the Society of American Foresters and the Forest Products Research Society, and was active in several civic organizations in Mercer County. (Courtesy of Donald G. Cuppett Jr.)

Five

Forestry Staff Adapts to Challenges

The dedication of the new wing on October 18, 1975, brought a crowd to the Forestry Sciences Laboratory in Gardner. Donald G. Cuppett Sr. invited timber industry officials from throughout the region to the event to meet the people behind the scientific innovations. (Courtesy of the US Forest Service.)

The remote work of logging is routinely far removed from the mingling of well-dressed folks at a dedication reception, but the scientific community at the Forestry Sciences Laboratory was absolutely committed to assisting the timber industry. (Courtesy of the US Forest Service.)

An old railroad caboose is shown here at the back of several railcars loaded with logs. Much of southern West Virginia was only accessible by rail until the latter part of the 20th century. Transportation was just one of the challenges facing the forestry scientists. (Courtesy of the US Forest Service.)

Louise Martin (left) presents a certificate of recognition to Early Moon, who grew up in a segregated part of the Arista coal-mining community. After completing his education, Moon took the job as paymaster at the Forestry Sciences Laboratory. A tireless community and public servant, Moon served several terms on the city council of Princeton, where he also served as mayor. (Courtesy of Jackie Rucker.)

The scientists of the Forestry Sciences Laboratory had the opportunity to usher in the computer age as the timber industry became high-tech. Judy F. Phillips (left), a computer technical assistant, is shown here with Dave Sonderman of the Forest Products Technology Program. (Courtesy of the US Forest Service.)

Of course, the goal of the scientists at the Gardner facility was to enhance the marketing possibilities for the timber industry. Since European colonists and African slaves arrived on the North American continent, lumber has been an important component of life. (Courtesy of the US Forest Service.)

Lumber continues to serve as a mainstay of the construction trades, and many cultures enjoy wood as a decorative element in offices and homes. Wood is a plentiful and renewable resource that enjoys popularity throughout the world. (Courtesy of the US Forest Service.)

Kenneth R. Whitenack (left), a mathematical statistician, is shown here working with Penny Lawson in one of several computer rooms in the facility. During its 53 years of service, the laboratory underwent many technological upgrades. (Courtesy of the US Forest Service.)

Bruce Anderson (right) played a vital role in the operations of the laboratory by serving as the economist at the Forestry Sciences Laboratory. He is shown with Robert Brisbind. (Courtesy of the US Forest Service.)

Forestry scientists from Mercer County traveled great distances in pursuit of their goals. Dan C. Todd photographed this balanced agricultural and forestry farm in Cooper Creek Valley near Margret, Georgia, in 1949. This farm remained in the same family for five generations. (Courtesy of the US Forest Service.)

This farm, along US Route 258 in Hertford County, North Carolina, was photographed by Leland J. Prater in 1955. The picture shows how forestry and farms can find balance throughout the Appalachian mountain region. (Courtesy of the US Forest Service.)

Dr. William G. Luppold served as project leader for the Forest Inventory & Analysis Group at the Forestry Sciences Laboratory, a group that included technologists, economists, mathematicians, and others. In recent years, Dr. Luppold continues to travel throughout the region to discuss the challenges facing its forests resources. (Courtesy of the US Forest Service.)

David G. Martens (left), forest products technologist, and Kathy Sherer examine a project. Martens and Sherer were both members of Luppold's project team. (Courtesy of the US Forest Service.)

While the scientists of the Forestry Sciences Laboratory were focused on developing new markets, they also strived to develop workplace safety strategies. Loading logs in forest conditions, as in this photograph, requires constant vigilance and awareness. (Courtesy of the US Forest Service.)

While loggers face challenging conditions in the forest, the movement of logs at a mill can also be dangerous. Forestry photographers and technicians gathered data in the field in order to find ways to improve safety through every stage of the logging process. (Courtesy of the US Forest Service.)

R. Edward Thomas (left) and Betsy S. Porterfield, both computer programmers, worked in the Research Work Unit, which was charged with increasing use of eastern hardwoods through better processing with improved technology. (Courtesy of the US Forest Service.)

David Emanuel (seated) and Jeff Palmer look over computer data. As work continued at the lab, the scientists became more reliant upon technology to track forestry production and safety data. (Courtesy of the US Forest Service.)

The railroad has always been an important customer of forest products. This photograph shows crossties ready to be placed in a treating cylinder in Salem, Virginia, while treated ties are being readied to move into storage. (Courtesy of the US Forest Service.)

Adzed bridge timbers are pictured in a seasoning yard at Salem. An adze is an ax-like tool used for dressing wood. Lumber plays an important role in the railroad industry. (Courtesy of the US Forest Service.)

Doris J. Nolley (right) is pointing out an illustration she prepared to Bruce G. Hansen, a forestry economist. Both were members of William Luppold's Forest Inventory & Analysis Group. (Courtesy of the US Forest Service.)

Donald Via (center) was maintenance mechanic, while Debbie Thompson (left) and Arnold Palmer served as laborers at the Forestry Sciences Laboratory. The three pose in front of the white oak cookie shown on page 21 of this book. (Courtesy of the US Forest Service.)

Charlie Gatchell, a forest products technologist, is shown conducting research. Gatchell also traveled throughout the region and took photographs to illustrate aspects of the timber industry to assist scientists in opening new markets and improving working conditions. (Courtesy of the US Forest Service.)

Joyce Coleman, secretary in the Improved Technology Work Unit, had a desk that illustrated the intensity and complexity of the work generated through the Forestry Sciences Laboratory. (Courtesy of the US Forest Service.)

Sometimes words only distract from the beauty of a photograph. Arnold F. Schultz took this picture of a farm in the Monongahela National Forest in Tucker County, West Virginia, in the spring of 1962. The farm was on Limestone Mountain Road at the head of Clay Lick Run. (Courtesy of the US Forest Service.)

Leland J. Parker took this aerial photograph of a Nicholas County farm near Beaver Creek in August 1962. This photograph was included in a series, likely in celebration of West Virginia's longstanding connection with the forest. (Courtesy of the US Forest Service.)

Leland J Prater's July 1946 photograph of a Centre County, Pennsylvania, farm shows a wheatfield being harvested with a combine. The farm was located west of State College, home of Penn State University. (Courtesy of the US Forest Service.)

A photograph can capture a moment in time, as in this June 1941 picture of a Vermont farm by B.W. Muir. The farm was on a side road off Highway 100 near the headwaters of the Tweed River. (Courtesy of the US Forest Service.)

This Leland J. Prater photograph, taken in August 1946, shows a farm in the George Washington National Forest near Powell's Fort Valley, Virginia. The farm is on a forested slope in a valley with the Massanutten Range in the background. (Courtesy of the US Forest Service.)

Leland J. Prater took this aerial photograph of cultivated fields along the Hocking River in Wayne National Forest in Ohio in October 1940. The highway is State Route 33. (Courtesy of the US Forest Service.)

Daniel J. Todd captured this May 1955 photograph of a rural North Georgia valley scene from State Highway 180 on the road to Brasstown Bald, Georgia's highest peak. The farm was located in the Chattahoochee National Forest. (Courtesy of the US Forest Service.)

This scene shows a good typical dairy farm setup. H.L. Shantz took this photograph in 1942. (Courtesy of the US Forest Service.)

Leland J. Prater took this aerial view of a Nicholas County, West Virginia, farm clearing in the forest near Beaver Creek in 1962. (Courtesy of the US Forest Service.)

This scenic landscape featuring shocks of corn and haystacks is located in the Monongahela National Forest at North Fork Valley, West Virginia. The photographer is unknown, but the picture was taken in 1938. (Courtesy of the US Forest Service.)

This farm is located along State Route 5 in Pendleton County, West Virginia, looking north toward Roaring Plains West Wilderness US Wilderness Area. E.S. Ship took this photograph in 1929. (Courtesy of the US Forest Service.)

This photograph was taken by B.W. Muir from Route 219 above Renick, West Virginia, showing a hill farm in Spring Creek Valley. Muir took this picture in June 1940. (Courtesy of the US Forest Service.)

Six

Modernization Opens New Opportunities

The USDA Forestry Sciences Lab is a beautiful sight year-round. In recent years, passersby might comment that the building looked like an elementary school. An appropriate response might be, "Possibly, elementary school buildings look like this." The innovative design and one-level easy access were a revolutionary concept in 1962. (Courtesy of the US Forest Service.)

The man third from left wearing coveralls and a hood and holding what appears to be a stopwatch appears to be Donald G. Cuppett Sr., then chief of the Forestry Sciences Laboratory, during a test of the guardrail post driver. The scientists at the lab came up with a marketing idea, designed or adapted the equipment necessary to make the product, and designed or adapted equipment to install the finished product. President Kennedy's idea of using the hardwood forests of the Appalachian mountain region to diversify and improve the economy was embraced by the Gardner scientists. (Courtesy of the US Forest Service.)

At the start of the 20th century, loggers clearcut most of the Appalachian Mountains' hardwood forest and left much of what was considered waste to rot on the forest floor. As a result, during the first decade of the 20th century, the region was beset by frequent and devastating forest fires. Congress took action in February 1905 to establish the US Forest Service to prevent forest fires and improve the vitality of all the forests in the United States. The scientists of the Forestry Sciences Lab focused their energies on finding useful ways to use secondary woods like the logs seen here, which were transformed into guardrail posts. (Courtesy of the US Forest Service.)

The scientists of the Gardner facility did not limit their footprint to just the Appalachian Mountains. This 1965 photograph shows loggers cutting timber for utility poles during the No. 2 Michigan River sale at the Routt National Forest in Steamboat Springs, Colorado. (Courtesy of the US Forest Service.)

Logs cut during the 1963 Ball Creek timber sale in the Kaniksu National Forest, on the Washington-Idaho border, are shown being loaded by a heel-boom loader. By studying practices used nationwide, scientists at the Gardner facility were able to recommend safety procedures that could be employed everywhere. (Courtesy of the US Forest Service.)

Large logs, like the one shown here being loaded during the Sam Hayton sale in Jefferson National Forest north of Walker Mountain in 1959, present additional safety challenges. Familiarity with existing logging practices provided the Gardner scientists with insights as to how to address challenges. (Courtesy of the US Forest Service.)

Of course, the goal of felling trees is getting the logs to a mill where they can be sawed, processed, and sold. Each step in that process requires skill, knowledge, and plenty of patience, as sawn lumber does not dry overnight. Sawmills like this one play a vital role in getting lumber ready for market. (Courtesy of the US Forest Service.)

By creating more markets for smaller logs and by removing good-sized timber waste from the forest floor, the logging industry was able to play a significant role in reducing the magnitude of some forest fires. Progress in opening secondary markets gave logging companies increased revenues, while the Gardner scientists worked to improve safety and increase pay for working lumberjacks. One of those markets came as a result of developing pallets for transporting large volumes of printed materials. The leadership at the Forestry Sciences Lab sold the concept to the US Postal Service, Sears, Roebuck & Co., and other businesses, including newspaper printers, and pallets like the ones being manufactured here gained widespread acceptance. (Courtesy of the US Forest Service.)

While the methods testing plant was a good first step for the USDA forestry scientists at Gardner to study innovations firsthand, they didn't have far to travel to examine real-world applications of processing practices. This photograph shows two workers removing logs from a steam vat at the Dean Veneer Plant in Princeton. (Courtesy of the US Forest Service.)

Logging in the Appalachian Mountains leaves the forest floor with a massive challenge in terms of erosion and sediment control. Timbering, surface mining, and even commercial or residential development can cause problems that adversely affect the forest's ability to generate regrowth. (Courtesy of the US Forest Service.)

While logs sent to lumber mills provide wood for construction, fine furniture manufacturing, shipping pallets, and many other useful products, the bark and other material are seldom used for those purposes. However, tree bark can be transformed into valuable mulch. (Courtesy of the US Forest Service.)

Lumber mill machines like the one shown here make short work of tree bark as they prepare logs of various sizes to be cut and sized by a saw. From 1907 to 1917, the Bluestone Lumber band saw left a 10- to 13-foot pile of sawdust over a large area on the site where the methods testing plant would be located. (Courtesy of the US Forest Service.)

The process of transforming the bark and scrap material into a mulch that can be used in many practical ways includes a few more steps prior to being sold to the public. First, it must be shredded to a size that is more useful. (Courtesy of the US Forest Service.)

Additional treatment may be necessary to mix in ecologically safe preservatives for use on residential, commercial, highway construction, industrial, or other applications. Some environmentally safe additives even result in the manufacture of mulch in several colors. (Courtesy of the US Forest Service.)

This photograph shows three different sizes of mulch as well as one that has been colored with a dark tint. Landscape artists, gardeners, farmers, construction companies, highway builders, and many others use mulch to aid in grass or flower growing or as an environmentally friendly way to control weeds. (Courtesy of the US Forest Service.)

Surface mining produces challenges in terms of forest regrowth due primarily to erosion. However, grass seeding with mulch can reduce soil loss and give a new growth of hardwoods an opportunity to take root. Foresters typically encounter problems, but providing soil stability is a good first step. (Courtesy of the US Forest Service.)

This photograph shows a site that has been seeded with grass to stabilize the soil. Practices that have halted erosion not only make the soil better prepared for forest regrowth but also provide habitat for wildlife including turkeys, deer, black bears, and others. (Courtesy of the US Forest Service.)

Loggers are loading Douglas fir logs using a Jennmar crane while harvesting timber from the Pole Creek No. 2 timber sale from the Beartooth National Forest on July 22, 1964. The Absaroka-Beartooth Wilderness is now part of the Custer-Gallatin National Forest in Montana. Logging in remote wilderness areas is difficult, but the scientists of the Forestry Science Lab sought to find solutions to every challenge faced by the timber industry, from finding the timber to harvesting and shipping it safely to creating new markets for forest products. (Courtesy of the US Forest Service.)

In any industry, and in every walk of life for that matter, safety is a constant concern. The crane operator and the hooker have established excellent eye contact, and despite the distractions that may be caused by the crane engine or the dozer working close by, they are able to reduce the risk of injury due to accident through good communication. The scientists of the USDA Forestry Sciences Lab worked to reduce lost-time injuries in the timber industry. (Courtesy of the US Forest Service.)

Some of the innovations that the scientists came up with include developing a practical system for weight-scaling logs to determine saw-log volume without costly measurements. They also developed the Solve program to help sawmill managers improve efficiency; a redesign for trucks for more efficient log transport; a method of pre-drying hardwoods that uses forced-air circulation and solar energy to supplement normal heat sources, speeding up the drying process to a third of the previous time; and much more. (Courtesy of the US Forest Service.)

The scientists of the Forestry Science Lab found it possible to produce construction-grade plywood from low-grade hardwood logs. They also worked closely with local industry on projects like this veneer slicer at the Dean Company plant in Princeton. (Courtesy of the US Forest Service.)

The scientists in Gardner worked closely with local lumber processing plants. Here, a worker is shown at the Dean Veneer Company in Princeton. The Dean Company worked hand-in-hand with the Forestry Sciences Lab to advance the cause of Appalachian hardwoods. (Courtesy of the US Forest Service.)

The Forestry Sciences Lab did extensive studies on injuries in the logging profession and recommended safety programs in logging and at sawmills that could pay for themselves with reduced worker-compensation insurance premiums, production delays, and material costs. (Courtesy of the US Forest Service.)

Along with reducing accidents, the forestry scientists recommended developing incentive programs along with other ways to increase work attendance. Their studies showed that the practices that were in place prior to 1975 actually did not reduce absenteeism. (Courtesy of the US Forest Service.)

Lab scientists assisted natural Christmas tree growers with information to help growers and dealers improve production planning and marketing strategies. Here, a woman poses with Christmas trees at Daniel Hale's plantation in Princeton. (Courtesy of the US Forest Service.)

Natural Christmas trees proved to be a successful business for many farmers in the Appalachian Mountains. The lab aided growers, distributors, retailers, and consumers while tracking sales and providing postseason accounting efforts to increase sales in the next year. Plus, more families got the opportunity to enjoy a natural Christmas tree. (Courtesy of the US Forest Service.)

Given a chance, the forest will naturally reclaim land that has been cleared for farming, logging, or surface mining. This abandoned farmland was photographed in July 1946 by Leland J. Prater from a scenic lookout near the Poe-Paddy Recreation Area (now Poe Paddy State Park) near State College, Pennsylvania. The houses, outbuildings, barn, and other evidence that families once called the place home are slowly returning to the forest. (Courtesy of the US Forest Service.)

Farm and forest can live in harmony, as shown in this August 1946 photograph by Leland J. Prater. Small family farms declined during the early 20th century as young people flocked to urban areas in search of jobs. Those jobs experienced a major setback in the 1930s after the stock market collapsed, throwing millions of people out of work and sending the nation into the Great Depression. People living on small family farms survived a little better than urbanites, because they could raise animals and gardens. However, those same family farms experienced harder times in the post–World War II years, when large farms with efficient mechanization changed the farming community. The farm pictured here was south of Harrisonburg, Virginia, in the George Washington National Forest. (Courtesy of the US Forest Service.)

Another photograph in a series by the US Forest Service, this picture was taken by Ben O. Todd of a farm in Cooper Creek valley near Margret, Georgia, in May 1949. Todd noted that the importance of the farm rested in its combination of farm and forestry. By way of illustrating the point, he wrote that the farm featured balanced agriculture with pasture on the lesser slopes, crops in the valley, and water in the stream. The same family had lived on and worked the farm for eight generations. The photographer told an inspiring story. (Courtesy of the US Forest Service.)

The US Forest Service photographers captured a moment of time in each of the photographs in this series. This photograph, taken in October 1940 by C.R. Hursh, shows a drainage system after scattered brush was removed and piled in gullies. After those tasks were finished, the farmer disked the land, fertilized, and planted rye. The farm was in the Bent Creek Experimental Forest, the oldest federal experimental forest east of the Mississippi River. The forest was established in 1925 and serves as home to the US Forest Service's Southern Research Station. Foresters at Bent Creek conduct research on silvacutural practices that aid in the rehabilitation of cutover, abused lands and promote sustainable forestry. Staff at Bent Creek also provide field demonstrations of forest management practices. (Courtesy of the US Forest Service.)

Almost everyone uses lumber in some aspect of their life, but few truly understand the complex processes that come into play before they sit on a wooden chair, walk across a wooden floor, or write at a wooden desk. The rural sawmill shown here could have supplied the beams that held together hundreds of homes, or much, much more. (Courtesy of the US Forest Service.)

Sawmill work can be dangerous, with logs weighing hundreds of pounds—in some cases tons—falling from cranes and bouncing into place. But the work of sawyers, lumberjacks, truckers, and everyone associated with everything from felling trees to hauling and processing lumber is part of a system that spans decades and helps make life on earth what it is today. (Courtesy of the US Forest Service.)

Seven

Mercer County Forestry Lab's New Mission

After consulting with Gov. Jim Justice, West Virginia Department of Commerce secretary Ed Gaunch appointed Charles T. "Tom" Cover director of the West Virginia Division of Forestry. Cover holds degrees from both Potomac State College and West Virginia University and has 44 years of experience in the wood industry. (Photograph by the author.)

Modern logging has undergone incredible change through the years. The traction assist tethered logging with running skyline system is shown here working on a mountain logging site in Wyoming County, West Virginia. The harvester cuts the trees, and the skyline tethering system drags logs to the top of a mountain for loading and transport to a sawmill. (Courtesy of the West Virginia Division of Forestry.)

Logging practices 50 to 60 years ago were limited in terms of the size and shape of timber as well as the methods of loading. Here, manpower was more directly involved in every aspect of logging. The crane operator and log rigger are literally on top of their job. (Courtesy of the US Forest Service.)

Tom Cover stands beside the cutting head of a large-scale logging operation. The operator maneuvers the head to encompass the base of the tree to fell the tree, then repositions to top the tree and stacks the trees in a line. Director Cover, like all of the men and women of the West Virginia Division of Forestry, are dedicated to protecting citizens, protecting the environment, and fighting forest fires wherever they emerge. (Courtesy of the West Virginia Division of Forestry.)

Three West Virginia Division of Forestry inspectors discuss the system with Line Mountain forester Gary Keaton (far left). Others shown include, from left to right, director Tom Cover, surface forester Brandon Hipps, and assistant regional forester Chris White. (Courtesy of the West Virginia Division of Forestry.)

Mat Bailey took this drone photograph of the mountaintop base of operations for the traction assist tethered logging with running skyline system, where all the logs are dragged for loading. (Courtesy of the West Virginia Division of Forestry.)

This May 1966 photograph by Richard L. Felton shows the J. Walter Wright logging operation in Washington County, near Abingdon, Virginia. Note the dilapidated structure beside the logging road. (Courtesy of the US Forest Service.)

In this February 1966 photograph by Richard E. Fenton, a loaded truck is shown on a roadway heading to a sawmill in the Abingdon area. The truck is hauling approximately 1,400 board feet of logs. Scientists at the USDA Forestry Sciences Laboratory developed new methods of more accurately determining timber payloads. (Courtesy of the US Forest Service.)

Clearcutting a mountain using a combination of the winch assist and harvest system and the traction assist tethered logging with running skyline system employed by Mountaineer Mechanized LLC may appear to be an affront to the environment, but this method leaves much less of the forest floor disturbed, leaves good topsoil for the seeds of a new forest to take root, and reduces the number of haul roads needed on a logging site. (Courtesy of the West Virginia Division of Forestry.)

Director Tom Cover estimated that it only takes about five workers to operate a traction assist tethered logging with running skyline system, and one of those employees must be a licensed forester. Cover said that Gary Keaton, Mountaineer Mechanized's forester on the Wyoming County job, is committed to minimizing disturbance as much as possible. (Courtesy of the West Virginia Division of Forestry.)

Along with protecting the environment, modern forestry is committed to producing the best possible lumber for a variety of applications. The February 1966 photograph by Richard H Fenton details the end-bored treated test ties intended to alleviate drying checks. Fenton took the photograph near Salem in Roanoke County, Virginia. (Courtesy of the US Forest Service.)

Another February 1966 Richard H. Fenton photograph shows a train loaded with untreated crossties in the Norfolk & Western yard at Salem. Heavy coal-country travel takes a toll on crossties, prompting the railway to conduct frequent tests and repair or replacement projects to keep trains moving smoothly and efficiently. (Courtesy of the US Forest Service.)

Since the 1830s, wood has been a standard component of railroad crossties. The vast majority are made of oak and hickory, but they can also be made from cherry, walnut, hemlock, redwood, and fir—all hardwoods indigenous to the Appalachian Mountains. The railroad crane shown here is placing treated ties in storage at Koppers Company in Salem. Photographer Richard H. Felton took this photograph in February 1966. Railroad ties have been treated with creosote, a substance made out of coal tar, since the early days of railroading, according to the American Wood Protection Association. (Courtesy of the US Forest Service.)

Mark Hundall, West Virginia Division of Forestry supervising forester for Wyoming County, observes the placement of the bucket on a modified John Deere excavator at a forestry project on a Wyoming County logging site. (Courtesy of the West Virginia Division of Forestry.)

The excavator bucket has to be secured properly in order to pull logs to the top of the traction assist tethered logging with running skyline system, where they are loaded for transport to sawmills. Soil disturbance is held to a minimum in this process, thus enhancing the potential for successful reforestation. (Courtesy of the West Virginia Division of Forestry.)

The forestry industry continues to address the challenge of getting logs to sawmills. Here a worker is using a modified forklift to unload a tandem-axle flatbed logging truck. Along with modifying equipment to handle various tasks, logging truckers have to remain vigilant while operating on diverse terrain. (Courtesy of the US Forest Service.)

Sawmills, like the one shown here, have always been one of the most important aspects of transforming timber into useful products that form an essential building block throughout the world. Timber is a sustainable natural resource that was used to build wooden ships that circumnavigated earth, and it played a small role in one lunar mission. (Courtesy of the US Forest Service.)

One operator works the controls of both the base of the traction assist tethered logging with a running skyline as well as the mountaintop loading area. Every step of a modern mechanized timber operation is designed to work efficiently while reducing any potential adverse impact to the forest floor. (Courtesy of the West Virginia Division of Forestry.)

The scale of a modern logging operation is difficult for many to understand, but the effort is concentrated. West Virginia Division of Forestry director Tom Cover said the goal is to use everything of the tree that can be used, from logs to peelers for pulpwood, oriented-strand board, and mulch. (Courtesy of the West Virginia Division of Forestry.)

Local foresters like the late Nelson Short commit a lifetime to protecting forests, homes, and communities from wildfires. After retiring from his day job as Mercer County Fire Board manager, Nelson passed a rigorous physical exam to qualify to battle fires out West. Nelson, who is shown here battling a Western forest fire, died on April 4, 2020, at the age of 75. (Courtesy of Amy Lester)

In February 2020, after nearly three years of continuous effort, the General Services Administration, National Park Service Historic Surplus Proprieties, US Forest Service, and West Virginia State Historic Preservation Office transferred the Forestry Sciences Lab to the Mercer County Commission. (Photograph by the author.)

The dedication stone near the main entrance to the facility pays homage to the commitment that Pres. John F. Kennedy made to serving the people of the Appalachian mountain region and to the US Forest Service. The fact that the lab's early leaders, Frank Longwood and Donald Cuppett, took that commitment to heart is reflected in every invention, project, and achievement that the scientists and technical support team accomplished in the site's 54-year history. That the laboratory was dedicated less than two weeks before President Kennedy's assassination and that West Virginia provided the national Christmas tree that was illuminated to signal the end to the nation's month-long period of mourning illustrate the spiritual bond that makes the site so special. (Photograph by the author.)

The Peaceful Valley Church on Cornbread Ridge Road was rebuilt on the site that once called Bluestone Lumber Company laborers to worship and that later served the residents of the Mercer County Poor Farm. Both the exterior and interior of the church are adorned with beautiful woodwork, perhaps paying homage to the church's origins. (Photograph by the author.)

The grave marker for Dominick Mosalinski is one of only two to indicate the final resting place of an individual who died while living at the poor farm. A few other graves have unmarked stones. The identities of only 65 people who died at the poor farm between 1928 and 1937 are known. Workers have estimated that from 250 to 300 unmarked graves are in the cemetery, which is in the process of being restored. (Photograph by the author.)

An unmarked opening into the 26-acre woodland leads to a beautiful hiking trail system featuring rock-lined trails, cliffs, and signs pointing out various flora along the way. The main trail leads to the Poor Farm Cemetery, but other trails are filled with other examples of woodland beauty. (Photograph by the author.)

One of the offshoot trails leads past several cliff outcroppings like the one pictured here, along with other examples of sylvan beauty. The cliff trail also includes a footbridge over a small ravine. (Photograph by the author.)

Most of the trail signage needs to be replaced, but this sign points the way to a woodland picnic area. The Mercer County Commission received a grant in the spring of 2020 from the National Coal Heritage Authority to restore signage and picnic tables and to acquire a battery-powered vehicle to transport ambulatory-challenged visitors to the picnic area and cemetery. (Photograph by the author.)

The picnic area includes a picnic table, several benches, and an open firepit. The clearing opens the typical canopy of trees and provides nighttime guests with an incredible view of the sky unencumbered by artificial lighting. (Photograph by the author.)

The Mercer County Commission has already started using the double-bay portion of the garage area to store personal protective equipment to aid the county's ongoing response to the COVID-19 pandemic, which is likely to persist until an effective vaccine is discovered. The inner five bays are currently being used for maintenance equipment. (Photograph by the author.)

In the early years after the Forestry Science Lab opened, this room in the garage was used to make custom-built furnishings for the interior of the lab. Many of the furnishings made here remain part of the lab. The Mercer County Commission is using this space to house the maintenance department and to store the ambulatory-challenged vehicle. (Photograph by the author.)

David G. Martens (left), a forestry products technologist, is shown in the lab's library with Sandra L. Corner, a secretary. Both Martens and Corner were members of the Forest Inventory and Analysist Group headed up by William Luppold. (Courtesy of the US Forest Service.)

The Mercer County Commission is working to restore the Forestry Sciences Lab library but also to use it as a community resource for small gatherings. In addition, the commission plans to save all the remaining photographs in a digital format to make them available to the public. (Photograph by the author.)

Some Mercer County employees have agreed to volunteer their time, talents, and green thumbs to rehabilitate the many flowerbeds surrounding the building. During the three-year stretch that the building was vacant, volunteers and some Mercer County staff kept the lawns surrounding the building mowed and trimmed. (Photograph by the author.)

Volunteers, staff, and Mercer County Day Report Center personnel tackled the task of removing trees and brush from the Poor Farm Cemetery and opening up the area to visitors. The work is ongoing, with several stumps needing removal, dead trees requiring felling, and grass needing planting, but the county commission is committed to the task. (Photograph by the author.)

These Mercer County employees put in a couple of overtime days to give the interior of the Forestry Science Lab a thorough cleaning. From left to right are Linnea Sanders, Sherri Howard, and Robin Hess. Sanders and Howard are both members of the maintenance staff, and Hess is a secretary with the Mercer County Commission. (Photograph by the author.)

While the US Forest Service staff cleared out most of the building, there were still plenty of cardboard boxes to be recycled and some filing cabinets and furnishings that needed moving. Donnie Thompson (left) and Scott Brookman, both members of the Mercer County Commission maintenance crew, are shown here clearing items from an office. This office is now occupied by the director of the Mercer County Economic Development Authority. (Photograph by the author.)

The Mercer County Economic Development Authority transformed this room into a boardroom and held its first meeting here on July 21, 2020. Since social distancing and face-covering requirements were in place due to the ongoing COVID-19 pandemic, several members of the Economic Development Authority Board participated via Zoom, while a few attended in person. The Economic Development Authority repurposed two tables from the Mercer County Day Report Center to serve in the boardroom. (Photograph by the author.)

Although there is nothing in the county commission records to verify this account, some old-timers have said that county employees salvaged the logs from the poor farm cabins built in the 1930s by workers from local CCC camps. Some have said county workers used the logs in the buildings associated with the 4-H camp in the county's Glenwood Park. (Photograph by the author.)

The Bluestone River flows within a few miles of the former forestry sciences lab. A nine-mile section of the Bluestone that flows through Summers County is the only river in West Virginia designated as a national wild and scenic river. Its origin is in Tazewell County, Virginia, but most of the remaining 55 miles of the river lie within Mercer County. In 2017, the Mercer County Commission established a committee to coordinate cleanup efforts on the river and its tributaries and also to develop a kayak and canoe water trail as well as a hiking and mountain bike trail, both non-motorized. The Bluestone Valley Trails group has been successful in receiving $300,000 from the West Virginia Department of Transportation's Recreational Trails Program, with funds from the Federal Highway Administration's Fixing America's Surface Transportation Act. Bluestone Valley Trails members hope to create a water and hiking trail along Brush Creek to connect the Gardner facility with the Bluestone River approximately four miles away. (Photograph by the author.)

Two avid trail hikers, Jeff Johnson (left), community development director with the Region 1 Planning & Development Council of the Appalachian Region Commission, and Mercer County attorney William S. "Bill" Winfrey, are shown here hiking an abandoned logging railroad on Camp Creek. Both are members of Bluestone Valley Trails. (Photograph by the author.)

The Bluestone River and its tributaries are becoming a popular destination for canoe and kayak enthusiasts, but the river and many of its tributaries still suffer pollution that has lingered from the time when Mercer County was a major coal-producing county. Chris Mullens, a 25-year veteran of Trout Unlimited, cleans debris from Crane Creek in Mercer County. Mullens is a member of Bluestone Valley Trails. (Photograph by the author.)

On its 20th anniversary in 1985, the Appalachian Region Commission commissioned artist Brett Johnson to create a work of art that would capture some of the commission's accomplishments. In the background of Johnson's artwork, Pres. John F. Kennedy represents the guiding force of the agency. Pres. Lyndon B. Johnson followed through with establishing the Appalachian Region Commission, and selected Franklin D. Roosevelt Jr. to serve as its first director. The two other men in the artwork, US senator John Sherman Cooper (left) and US senator Jennings Randolph, were at the forefront of the commission, but President Kennedy's dream continues for states throughout the Appalachian region. Certainly, the leadership and staff of the US Forest Service's Forestry Sciences Laboratory in Gardner took the message and mission to heart. During the lab's five-plus decades of service, the scientists and staff made differences that had both immediate and long-term ramifications. That message will live on as the Mercer County Commission transitions the site into a new public purpose. (Courtesy of West Virginia Region One, Appalachian Region Commission.)

INDEX